Leadership
IS NOT ABOUT
Y(*)OU

Kate!
Glad we're on the
same team. :)
-tim

TIM MILBURN

LEADERSHIP IS NOT ABOUT YOU / Tim Milburn
ISBN 978-1493554652

www.leadershipisnotaboutyou.com

For Kenton Lee

*You have leadership written all over you
and you're a great leader because
you know it's not about you.*

CONTENTS

"If your internal compass remains focused on the needs and concerns of those around you, there's a good chance you'll be pointed in the right direction."

-- Victor Lipman --

INTRODUCTION
IT'S NOT ABOUT YOU...BUT IT STARTS WITH YOU

THE TITLE OF THIS BOOK IS A PUNCHLINE.

Not to the end of a joke, but to a principle.

I addressed the first part of the principle in my previous book, *Leadership Starts With You*. I couldn't write this book until I wrote that one. All of the lessons in *Leadership Is Not About You* make a lot more sense when you take the time to invest in the ideas in *Leadership Starts With You*.

It's simple really. **Leadership starts with you but it is not about you.**

The premise of this book is about leadership that focuses on others after you have focused on yourself. The way YOU lead YOU affects the way YOU lead OTHERS. And it plays a key role in whether OTHERS are willing to follow YOU.

If you have not read *Leadership Starts With You*, I encourage you to put this book down and begin with that one. Don't worry. I'll be here when you get back.

For those of you who might be a little short on time (or cash), here's a snapshot of what I mean when I say leadership starts with you.

Leadership starts with one person — you. It starts there because any attempt to lead others well without leading yourself well typically ends up causing a great deal of frustration.

This isn't about selfishness. In fact, it's the first and most necessary step toward selflessness.

The leadership of yourself is the foundation for any effort you make in the leadership of others.

The way you lead yourself helps others determine if you are a leader worth following. They are asking the question: *If I can't trust YOU to lead YOU well, then how can I trust YOU to lead ME well?*

WHAT DOES IT MEAN TO LEAD YOURSELF WELL?
It begins by learning to take responsibility, both for your choices and the consequences of those choices. You don't always have to be right, but you do have to be honest.

Leading yourself first means you work hard to make good decisions about your own life. Small and big decisions that accumulate. Decisions that end up determining the kind of person you are going to be and the kind of things you are going to do.

You develop discipline in your life. Others are watching the effect your decisions have on your actions and behavior. They can see and feel the ripples your actions create. Over time, people learn whether they can trust you based on your consistency and your character.

You grow your character through your daily decisions and your response to those decisions.

Too many people have lost the opportunity to lead others as a result of leading themselves poorly. They had to step down or were removed from leadership.

How many of us can name someone whose influence came to a crashing halt because of a moral failure, fatal flaw, or lack of discipline in his or her life?

Please, take the time to build your own life into something

worth following. Then we'll be ready to move on to the next step — adding others into the mix.

I'M A BIG FAN OF CHALLENGE COURSES. They are a great way to connect a group of people you're trying to form into a team. The high elements take courage and push people out of their comfort zones. But it's the low elements where you get a good feel for the dynamics in the group.

One of the low elements we use is called The Wall (because...well...it's a wall). The Wall stands about 12-15 feet high. The goal is to get your entire team over the wall. There's a ledge on the opposite side of the wall to stand on once you climb over. It enables someone to lean over the top of the wall and reach down to assist others.

Once again, the goal is to get the entire team over the wall.

I love to watch as one or two people begin to take a leadership role. It's not that they bark orders or tell everyone what to do. **They simply put themselves in the best position possible to get the entire team over the wall** (POP QUIZ: ARE YOU IN THE BEST POSITION TO DO THIS FOR YOUR TEAM?). Sometimes, they'll go first and stand on the ledge to pull people over the wall. Sometimes they stay on the ground and push people up and over the wall. They never seem that concerned about getting themselves over the wall. It's more about getting everyone over the wall.

You can tell who the leader of a group is by his or her shoulders.

The leader is the person whose shoulders bear the responsibility.

You see, leadership begins with responsibility — the responsibility for one's decisions and the responsibility for the team's direction. If all you want to do is get yourself over the wall, you're not the kind of leader most people are looking for.

The effective leaders put the people around them on their shoulders. I've seen those who want to be the leader because they want to be on the shoulders of the people around them. They want the recognition. They want the accolades. If that's your motive — if you want the spotlight — then maybe you should try out for American Idol.

LEADERS TAKE THE RESPONSIBILITY TO PUT THEMSELVES IN THE BEST POSITION FOR THEIR TEAM TO SUCCEED.

Sometimes they have to push and sometimes they have to pull. They know it will take a group effort to accomplish their objective. You aren't the leader if you just get yourself over the wall. Besides, that's not much of an accomplishment.

Some people enter into leadership hoping to attract followers like some sort of "pied piper." They mistakenly think those around them will automatically do what they say and respect them because they're in the front of the line (and they have the flute). True leadership — the essence of what people long for and desperately want to follow — entails an appropriate level of humility that brings out the best in others.

True leaders possess the capacity to recognize that leadership is about serving others instead of being served.

Jim Collins, in his book, *Good To Great*, illustrates this idea in a way that I'll sum up here. When it's all about you as a leader, you'll look in the mirror, beat your chest, and tell yourself how good you are when things go well. When something goes wrong, you look out the window and blame those around you. But, when you understand that leadership is not about you, you'll look out the window and give those around you the credit when things go well. When things go wrong, you humbly look in the mirror and ask yourself, "What could I have done differently."

YOU CAN INSPIRE YOUR FOLLOWERS THROUGH THE OPPORTUNITIES YOU HAVE TO GET BEHIND THEM. You are in a position to challenge them to live up to their potential and do their best. You can help others realize their unique gifts and talents and skills and passions. **You will find that people follow your leadership because you serve their needs rather than strut your stuff.**

When you understand that leadership is not about you, you'll put the needs of others before your own. You'll make others feel better about themselves when they're in your presence. You'll connect them to other people and projects where they'll discover a greater sense of purpose and meaning in their lives.

When it's not about you, you understand that it takes giving away all you can for others instead of taking all you can for yourself. **Your leadership position is a platform.** You get to choose how you use it. Will you be selfish or selfless?

In *Leadership Starts With You*, I encourage you to spend

time investing in yourself so you can be at your best. When you develop that discipline, it's time to take the next step and begin to lead others in a way that truly makes a difference.

This book is a collection of ideas and principles designed to help you become the kind of leader that others want to follow when they don't have to. One who leads through inspiration, influence, and example. The kind of leader who is motivated by the idea of guiding and growing a group of people toward a better future.

It seems so obvious, but the first criterion for any leader is that he or she should have the desire to lead. And by "lead," I don't mean that the would-be leader simply wants to be in charge or stand as the figurehead.

True leadership is about *service, accountability* and *sacrifice.*

Any leader who wants to inspire the best in others accepts all three of these things willingly.

This whole thing starts with you. But at some point you come to the realization it's not really about you. I know...it feels like a paradox.

According to Dictionary.com, paradox is defined as *a statement or proposition that seems self-contradictory or absurd but in reality expresses a possible truth.*

Paradox or not, the type of leadership that starts with you but isn't about you, is leadership worth following.

I would tweak the dictionary definition just a little bit. Instead of saying this paradox *expresses a possible truth*, I believe this paradox is *a truth with all kinds of possibilities.* As long as we're willing to learn and grow, we will discover ways to make a difference in the lives of others. Enjoy the journey as we unpack these possibilities together.

Let's begin.

✳ ✳ ✳
THE RHODIUM RULE REVISITED

Did you read the word "rule" and want to skip this chapter? I hope it doesn't scare you. It's a good rule. I know because I created it (and I don't like rules). It was inspired by the Golden Rule. But it's different. Very different.

Most people recognize the Golden Rule when they hear it. Although "most people" doesn't include my youngest daughter. I asked her if she knew the Golden Rule. She nodded in affirmation. "It's monkey see, monkey do."

Sigh. Thanks sweetheart...here are some lovely parting gifts.

YOU CAN APPLY MY RULE TO YOUR LIFE TODAY AND SEE THE EFFECTS IMMEDIATELY. It's at the heart of leadership that starts with you but isn't about you. One of the differences between my rule and the Golden Rule is *who* it starts with. The Golden Rule starts with an emphasis on others. It states, "Do unto others as you would have them do unto you."

My rule starts with an emphasis on *you*.
I call it **The Rhodium Rule.**

I know you're probably wondering *What the heck is Rhodium?* I didn't know either. But you can learn a lot of cool stuff on the internet.

Rhodium is one of the elements on the periodic table (atomic number 45) and is considered to be a precious metal. In fact, it's often used to protect other precious metals. It keeps things from corroding. That's handy, but it's not why I named my rule after it.

I asked my friend who is chemistry professor (we should all have a friend like that), "What's so special about Rhodium?" He looked at me and said, "It's more precious than gold...and it's a catalyst." Wow. It's rare and it gets things going. That confirmed it for me!

Here it is — the Rhodium Rule:

Do unto yourself what will inspire the best in others.

Do you see the difference between this rule and the Golden Rule? The Rhodium Rule encourages you to start with yourself. It's the motive behind what you do to you that makes it about others.

The way you personally live, work, grow and lead can serve as an example that encourages the best in others.

YOU WORK HARD TO CREATE THE BEST VERSION OF YOURSELF SO YOU CAN INSPIRE OTHERS TO BE THE BEST THEY CAN BE. It's not about dictating your demands or forcing people into a certain mold of your choosing. You don't use your power or position to manipulate people. You use your own example to motivate people.

You model what it looks like to be disciplined, productive, and trustworthy out of a desire for others to exhibit those same characteristics in their own lives.

When you apply the Rhodium Rule to your life, you seek the best for others by striving to be the best you can be.

For me, the word "best" simply means *reaching toward your potential at any given moment.*

When you follow the Rhodium Rule, you lead yourself in a way that actually makes other people's lives better. You push into your potential in order to inspire others to do the same. You rise above mediocrity in your own life to show others that it's possible for them as well.

If you adopt the Rhodium Rule as a guiding principle it could revolutionize your leadership. By adopt, I mean apply it in your daily life. You can't just believe it. You have to behave according to it. Here's what I mean:

1. YOU HAVE TO DO SOMETHING.

The Rhodium Rule is based on action. You can't simply nod your head in affirmation. It must be more than belief. It requires a certain type of behavior. It's you DOING (everyday-habitual-life-enhancing behaviors) your best to lead yourself well.

2. YOUR MOTIVE: DO YOUR BEST TO INSPIRE THE BEST.

Lots of people are into self-improvement for improvement's sake. I applaud that. When you apply the Rhodium Rule to your life, it takes self-improvement to the next level.

Your motive to improve and grow isn't solely for your own gain. Leaders who are in it for themselves are easy to identify. But we are all inspired by those who are willing to work hard and then show us how to do the same thing in our own lives.

3. YOUR ACTIONS MUST BE OBSERVABLE.

Like the Golden Rule, you cannot *set* an example unless people can *observe* your example. The Rhodium Rule only works when you live your life out loud in front of others, especially those people whom you are leading. This requires authenticity and transparency.

The Rhodium Rule works in both the good and not-so-good moments of life. The people around you are watching how you respond to life, especially those times when life doesn't go as you might have hoped.

Your reaction and response to mistakes, failures, blunders, and your own weaknesses will help others know how to handle their own.

The Rhodium Rule isn't about being a perfect person. It's about being a person who is making progress.

Here's an example from my own life. I remember lashing out at one of my student leaders because he was pushing for a proposal that I thought was ill-advised and poorly timed. While I had years of experience over him and might have been right, I confronted him poorly. I can honestly say I was not following the Rhodium Rule at that moment. When I had some time to reflect on the situation (as well as hear from a couple other people about how stunned he was by my verbal tongue-lashing), I called him into my office. He hesitantly agreed to come in and sit down.

"Before we say anything else, I need you to know how sorry I am for the way I spoke to you," I said. "I was completely wrong in the way I handled the situation and I need to ask for your forgiveness."

He paused for a moment. Then he looked at me and said, "I appreciate your apology. I didn't expect to hear that from you today. I am glad you brought me in to talk."

At no point in the conversation did I offer any type of excuse for my actions. I took full responsibility for my outburst. I didn't blame it on anyone else or on the circumstances. I offered a clear, heartfelt apology.

In that moment, the Rhodium Rule was working. This was a situation where I needed to lead myself well by publicly owning up to my own failure. In doing so, I was setting an example of what an honest apology looked like. I'm reminded of how many times I told my own children to say

"I'm sorry" like you mean it. It's easier for them to do that when they've seen it authentically modeled by someone else.

I wish I had kept my cool when I initially confronted this student. But I didn't and I had to own my mistake. I humbly came back to him and shared my regret and my apology. The Rhodium Rule was applied to this situation. I wanted to be the type of person who took responsibility for myself (and my mistakes). I wanted this rule to benefit this student.

Think about the ways you can apply the Rhodium Rule to your own life. In what areas are you going to strive to be a GOOD example? An example others can see and imitate?

You need to make an investment in YOU so that you're better able to be an influence on OTHERS.

✳ ✳ ✳
BEYOND OBLIGATION

A leadership position has certain responsibilities and requirements. The requirements are typically listed in the job description that goes along with the position. When you decide to serve in a leadership position, you accept the responsibility of completing all of the tasks, projects, and outcomes that are required in the job description.

The job description is your obligation as a leader.

The job description is there so that you know what you have to do. You serve in a leadership position in order to fulfill the duties the position requires. Of course, there is a style of leadership that allows a person to do whatever he or she wants in a position. It's called a dictatorship. While dictatorship is considered a form of leadership, it typically doesn't go well for the followers or end well for the leader.

FORTUNATELY, THERE IS A PLACE IN LEADERSHIP FOR DOING WHAT YOU WANT TO DO AND NOT JUST WHAT YOU HAVE TO DO. But it only comes after you fulfill the responsibilities and requirements of your job description.

I call this place the opportunity that exists beyond obligation.

You will be evaluated on your ability to meet the demands and deadlines of the work that is required of you. But I want to encourage you to live beyond the minimum requirements of your position.

DON'T LET YOUR JOB DESCRIPTION SET THE BAR FOR YOU. There are incredible opportunities that exist on the other side of your obligations. When you truly believe that leadership is not about you, you'll find the little extra beyond each obligation. You'll see opportunity.

Opportunities are the extra ways you impact and influence the lives of others.

Something very special happens when you begin to do a little bit more than what's required. I know you are committed to follow through on your obligations. I want you to take it a step further. I believe you can make an even greater contribution.

Start with your OBLIGATIONS, but be on the lookout for OPPORTUNITIES.

Obligation gets you going.
OPPORTUNITY GET YOU NOTICED.

Obligation lists your tasks.
OPPORTUNITY LIFTS YOUR TALENTS.

Obligation is what you have to do.
OPPORTUNITY IS WHAT YOU WANT TO DO.

You can complete all of your obligations and people will thank you for doing your job. I want to challenge you to move through your obligations into the realm of opportunity. That's where people will recognize you for making a difference.

IF ALL YOU FOCUS ON ARE THE OBLIGATIONS OF YOUR POSITION, YOU MIGHT BE TEMPTED TO DO THE LEAST THAT'S REQUIRED FOR THE MOST YOU CAN GET OUT OF IT. But if you complete your obligations with an eye for opportunity, you'll find ways to do what's meaningful for the most others can get out of it.

One of the main reasons people don't take the time to look for opportunity beyond obligation is fear. They're afraid to put themselves out there. They're afraid they'll make a mistake or look foolish. They don't want to do anything to stand out so they stick to the job description.

Some people hide behind the tasks of their leadership position because they're afraid to admit that no one is actually following them.

They haven't connected with those around them. They haven't made the most of the opportunities to impact the lives of others. It has to be difficult when you're in a leadership position but no one actually thinks you're a leader.

THE IMPACT GRAPH

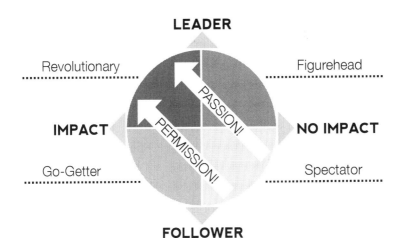

I created the IMPACT graph to help people identify how effective they felt in their leadership position. I wanted them to begin to think about the differences between those who make an impact and those who don't.

The x axis measures *Impact vs No Impact*. The y axis measures *Follower vs Leader*.

I've labeled each of the four quadrants:

Follower/No Impact = *Spectator*
Leader/No Impact = *Figurehead*
Follower/Impact = *Go Getter*
Leader/Impact = *Revolutionary*

I use this graph to illustrate the journey many take toward effective leadership. I want to inspire people to move from *spectator* to *revolutionary*. It's not enough to just show up and fill a spot. Those who do the least that's required of them live on the *No Impact* side of the graph. They don't want to take responsibility and aren't concerned with moving people forward.

PEOPLE MOVE TOWARD THE *IMPACT* SIDE OF THE GRAPH WHEN THEY START TO PUT THEIR HEART AND SOUL INTO WHAT

THEY'RE DOING. Whether you are in a position of leadership or not, you can make a difference. The secret is this:

The more you find the opportunity beyond obligation, the greater impact you will make.

The world is full of people who get up every morning and do the same thing they saw the last person do. They go through the motions and live with the lowest of expectations.

Are you going to be different? When you understand that leadership is not about you, you'll look for ways to move into the realm of opportunity - to do a little more than what's required. Don't do it out of selfishness or greed, do it out of selflessness and the desire to make a difference in the lives of others.

THE *REVOLUTIONARIES* OF THE WORLD EXCEED EXPECTATIONS. They've identified a problem and taken the responsibility to solve it. They impact others because they serve others. They don't settle for the status quo. They paint a picture of a better future. It's so compelling that others can't wait to be a part of it. We call that vision!

One more thing about the IMPACT graph. A person moves from *No Impact* to *Impact*, and from *Follower* to *Leader* through their passion and the permission of others.

Your passion — doing the things you love to do — will pull you toward leadership opportunities. When you take the time to serve others beyond what's required of you, they will give you the permission to lead them. Sometimes that happens through an election or selection process. Often, it happens because people are drawn to someone who is going places.

The people who are going places do what's expected...and then some.

Did you hear those three words? And...then...some...

This is the path to excellence. You are pushing yourself beyond obligation. You give a little more energy and creativity to the opportunities you see each day.

The difference between ordinary and extraordinary is the "extra." And...then...some...

• If you procrastinate, you will have to settle for

obligation instead of opportunity.

- If you just do what's required, you will have to settle
  for obligation instead of opportunity.
- If it's all about you, you will have to settle for
  obligation instead of opportunity.

The path to opportunity is paved with those things that will inspire the best in others. Or to put it another way...

Your greatest opportunities will occur when you focus more on the people you work with than the work itself.

Have you seen the professional ball player who was an incredible athlete and a horrible coach? Skill alone doesn't qualify one for leadership. It's the ability to connect with others and inspire them toward greatness that makes a leader worth following. **The moment it becomes more about showing off your own skill than it is about serving their needs, your opportunities to lead will diminish.**

The leaders who make the greatest impact understand how meaningful the opportunities are beyond one's obligations. Howard Hendricks said, "You can impress people at a distance, but you can impact them only up close." It's when you draw close to those around you that the opportunities start to reveal themselves.

Too many leaders go through the motions. But not you! No, you will go beyond obligation. Because now you know. You can take a simple, routine task and turn it into an opportunity to make things a little bit better. You not only want to do your best, you want to inspire others to be better as well.

Take a moment and reflect on all of the tasks you HAVE to do in your leadership position. These are important components of your role. Do them and do them well.

But let's take it a step further.

How can you expand some of those obligations into opportunities? How can you go beyond what you HAVE to do and incorporate some ideas of what you WANT to do?

It's in the opportunities where you'll make the greatest impact in the lives of others.

✳ ✳ ✳
MOVING FROM YOURS TO OURS

YOU CARRY THE VISION FOR THE TEAM BECAUSE YOU'RE THE LEADER. This means you have a clear and compelling picture of a better future. You can actually see it in your mind. You help those around you see that we can't stay *here* because we have to get to *there*.

Vision is a funny thing. It's just an idea. It's a reality that doesn't exist yet. It hasn't actually happened. But it could. It could happen if you find a way to get those around you to buy into this vision for a better future and start working toward it.

For that reason, vision can't be the sole property of the leader. **Personal vision must become shared vision.** You want those around you to know it and own it.

One way this happens is by giving them the **Y**.

The way you take a vision that's *yours* and make it *ours* is to give those around you the **Y**. Take the "y" off of yours and hand it out. When you give the "y" away, *yours* becomes *ours*.

Y = WHY

Do you see what I did there? This is more than an exercise in spelling or a play on words. Those around you need to know WHY something is important before they'll own it for themselves.

People don't like to be told what to do. You might be the boss, but no one enjoys being bossed around. Even as kids we felt the need to know the WHY. When someone asked us to do something, we'd want to know why. The response of *because I said so* just sounded like an authoritative demand that lacked a good reason (I'm trying to count how many times I said that as a parent).

Unfortunately, many leaders only focus their time and energy trying to get people to do the what, where, when, and how that's necessary to accomplish the vision. When you do this, you run the risk of keeping the vision *yours* instead of *ours*.

It's the WHY that captures people's hearts. It motivates and energizes them to do their best work. **PEOPLE WILL BUY INTO AND COMMIT TO THE VISION WHEN THEY UNDERSTAND AND BELIEVE IN THE *WHY* OF THE VISION.**

Effective leaders connect this WHY to the passions, needs, and desires of those around them. They help people see themselves in this picture of a better future.

They don't just tell them it's better, they explain WHY this vision for the future is better than where they're at right now.

You will leave those around you in the dark when you *decide* on a vision but don't take the time to *describe* the vision. WHEN YOU DON'T DESCRIBE THE VISION IN TERMS OF *WHY*, YOU ROB THE VISION OF IT'S EMOTIONAL POWER.

Here are FIVE observations I've made when it comes to turning yours into ours:

1. When you ask someone to do something, tell them WHY it's important. That's empowering.

2. WHY is a stronger motivation than WHAT.

3. People form groups and causes around WHY.

4. You will get more extra effort when you give the WHY than you will if you only give the WHAT.

5. If people know WHY something is important, they'll
surprise you with HOW they accomplish it.

You connect those around you to the vision on a deeper
level when you give them your WHY. They begin to see what
they're doing as significant, meaningful, and relevant.

And you'll know they've taken ownership of the vision and
committed themselves to it when they start to talk about
this shared vision and refer to it as *OURS*.

LISTENING IS YOUR GREATEST COMMUNICATION SKILL

I've watched a lot of capable people shy away from a leadership position because they had a fear of public speaking. In their mind, they thought effective leaders were the ones who gave speeches. That's a myth.

Your greatest communication skill as a leader is not your ability to speak, it's your ability to listen.

I like the way my friend Ryan Roberts puts it, "The best leaders hit the ground listening."

AS A LEADER, YOU'VE GOT TO LISTEN OR YOU'LL SOON END UP WITH PEOPLE WHO HAVE NOTHING INTERESTING TO SAY ANYMORE. Why should they speak up if they know they won't be heard?

In one ear and out the other is more than a cliche'. It's a sign of poor leadership.

You heard them. You nodded your head. You even recited

back to them what they just said. But listening did not take place.

What was missing was the ability to understand what was being said. That's why the best listeners approach a conversation with a learner's lean. THEY DON'T SIMPLY TRY TO HEAR THE WORDS, THEY TRY TO GRASP THE MEANING.

Things like eye contact, body language, focusing on a person (and not your cell phone), and looking at non-verbals are more than posturing. They're tools that aid in the quest for understanding.

It's not enough to simply hear someone. There's a lot of loud voices out there scrambling for attention. The question is: Are we hearing what they're saying or are we hearing what we want to hear?

Objectively listening (seeking to understand without preconceived notions) is one of the hardest things to do as a leader. In all of the conversations you have, you are listening to others through the filter of your own life. This includes your experiences, your thoughts, and your own agendas.

WE HEAR THROUGH OUR OWN DEFINITIONS OF WORDS. We hear through our perceptions and our intellect. We enter every conversation with a set of assumptions. It is difficult as a leader to do what Stephen Covey has recommended – to seek first to understand, then to be understood.

LISTENING, REALLY LISTENING, TAKES TIME. When things get busy, we tend to listen a lot less. Too many leaders get caught up in focusing on all of the tasks and tactical challenges of leadership. **Yet, you make a tremendous impact and gain credibility as a leader when you connect with those around you on an emotional and heart level.** Those types of conversations take time.

IF YOU WANT TO GET BETTER AT LISTENING, YOU WILL NEED TO GET BETTER AT ASKING QUESTIONS. Leaders engage those around them not so much by the answers they give, but by the questions they ask.

Leadership is not about always being right, it's about **finding the right answers.** And finding the right answers can only come when you take the time to listen to others. The reason is simple: You only know what you know and you don't know what you don't know. You must ask questions — and lots of them — to gain more information, learn more and hear other perspectives.

By listening to the responses of others, you help them see that you don't have all of the answers. And you inspire them to help you find the best answers.

THOSE AROUND YOU ARE MORE APT TO LISTEN TO YOU IF YOU'VE TAKEN THE TIME TO LISTEN TO THEM. Getting people to listen to you is like respect — both need to be earned. You take the time to connect with their heart before you ever ask them to do something. When you make those connections, people are more willing to hear your ideas. They will listen to you when they feel listened to.

Before you enter into a conversation with someone, ask yourself: *How do I want to make this person feel?* Put yourself in his or her shoes. Listen with all of your senses. Every conversation is an opportunity to inspire people.

LISTEN WITH THE GOAL OF UNDERSTANDING. Listening isn't simply a chance to catch your breath so you can start talking again. When you understand that leadership is not about you, the way you listen to those around will communicate louder than words.

✳ ✳ ✳
FIND A REASON TO CELEBRATE

I could tell our team was tired. We had just gone through a whirlwind of events. It seemed like we had lived in our conference room for the last month, preparing for each activity that fell on the heels of the last one. With every successful event, our team felt a little more depleted.

Finally, the crazy, insane, busy period was over. We were all sprawled out across the tables and chairs, exhausted from our furious pace. One of the members of our team leaned back in his chair and sighed these words.

We don't party enough.

That was a good reminder. Not that we needed to take something or do something to numb our senses. In that moment he helped us all realize we had lost one of the most meaningful parts of being on a team. We weren't having fun anymore. We hadn't spent enough time celebrating what we actually accomplished together.

IF YOU'RE LEADING A GROUP OF PEOPLE, IT CAN BE EASY TO FALL INTO A ROUTINE OF JUST DOING THE WORK. We push those around us to achieve goals, complete tasks, and do their jobs.

But you know what happens? In our efforts to keep going, we forget to stop.

We wrongly assume that celebrations are meant for the end of the year, not in the middle of our work week. It's one of those things that sits at the bottom of our priority list.

What if we changed that? What if you and your team put as much creativity into planning your celebrations as you do in planning and implementing your events? That's the kind of team I'd love to be on.

You know what gets in the way of our celebrations? Evaluation. And I like evaluation (maybe that makes me a glutton for punishment). But that helps me make my point. I think we go about evaluating our work the wrong way.

Most teams tend to sit around the table at the end of an event or activity and take time to evaluate. In our effort to improve, we'll spend the majority of our time trying to figure out how to fix all of the things that went wrong. We start with the wrong and try to make it right.

What if we turned that upside down? By all means, fix the glaring errors that occurred. But let's change the focal point of your evaluation. **I am suggesting you take two-thirds of your time and lead your team in the process of acknowledging what went right and thinking about how to improve in those areas.**

STOP AND CELEBRATE HOW WELL YOU PERFORMED AND THE RESULTS YOU ACHIEVED. Pass out credit where credit is due. Highlight the highlights. Give people awards and accolades and a steady flow of high fives.

In *Leadership Starts With You*, I challenged you to personally work on improving in the area of your strengths and delegating in the area of your weakness. If that principle works on a personal level, just think about how powerful it will be on your team.

I know it might be difficult to change your mindset here.

Perhaps you were conditioned just like I was. It started when we brought our report card home from school. You remember, it was the one where we did well in "most" of our classes. But there was one or two classes where we struggled. We weren't proud of that grade and we weren't looking forward to having our parents see it.

There it was, a lone "D" surrounded by an "A", a couple of "B's", and a "C." All we could see was the "D." And in my case, so did my parents. They would gloss over all of the other grades and focus in on that "D".

They might have said something like, "Well, these are pretty good grades but what happened here?" or "D's aren't acceptable in this house!" or "What are we (that meant me) going to do to get this grade up?"

Most of that conversation focused on the "D" and not much time on the other "better" grades. And we've carried that same mindset into the way we lead our teams. We think improvement can only come in the areas we do poorly in.

If we spend all of our time focused on fixing failures, it leaves little time for acknowledging and celebrating victories.

By all means, learn and grow from the mistakes, but don't miss your chance to applaud those things that went really well. Congratulate the work that's great.

CELEBRATION IS A HUGE MOTIVATOR. It inspires others to perform and to continue to perform at a high level. Somebody a lot smarter than me put it very succinctly: What gets rewarded gets done.

Tom Peters, management and leadership guru said it this way, "Celebrate what you want to see more of." This means we need to put rewards and celebration on the agenda.

THE MOST EFFECTIVE TEAMS HAVE LEARNED HOW TO DO MORE OF WHAT WORKS AND LESS OF WHAT DOESN'T. One of the ways to encourage what works is to celebrate it when it happens. If you wait until the end of the year you miss out on an opportunity to make your team even better right now.

Just look at the positive impact celebration can have on your team:
- Celebrations make people feel like they did something significant.
- Celebrations promote teamwork because people bond when they accomplish something together.
- Celebrations affirm the goals and values of the team.

- Celebrations are a positive way to communicate the team's priorities.
- Celebrations create momentum.
- Celebrations strengthen relationships.

Celebrations make you hit the pause button in your routine.

They energize your team toward future success.

As you implement celebration into the flow of your work, consider the following:

1. THERE IS NO RIGHT WAY TO CELEBRATE.

Tailor your celebrations around what your team will enjoy. Don't get stuck celebrating in the same way every time unless you are intentionally trying to create some type of tradition.

Experiment with a variety of ways to keep things exciting and unexpected. Celebrations can range from a thank you note to a large-scale event.

2. WHENEVER THERE IS A SIGNIFICANT ACCOMPLISHMENT OR TRANSITION, TAKE TIME TO CELEBRATE.

Transitions are difficult. Celebrating what went well helps

bring closure and builds momentum for the next thing.

3. MAKE SURE CELEBRATIONS HAVE A PURPOSE.

While it's fun to throw a party, celebrations are most effective when they happen for a reason. Be very clear about who or what is being celebrated. Meaningless celebration will only dilute the effectiveness of other celebrations that do need to happen.

4. MAKE SURE CELEBRATIONS HAVE A PERSONAL FEEL TO THEM. REWARD PEOPLE SPECIFICALLY.

Celebrating a team effort is important. In the midst of this remember that personal recognition is very powerful, especially when it's tied to something that helps the team be successful.

5. ALLOCATE RESOURCES FOR CELEBRATIONS AND REWARDS.

Celebrations don't have to cost a lot of money. But if you make celebrations part of your team's culture, make sure you allocate resources to make these times meaningful. The level of celebration should match the amount of work and effort that went into creating the success.

The song gets it right: Celebrate good times! Come on!

LEADERSHIP AS AN ACT OF SERVICE

What if you viewed leadership as a platform for service rather than a position for power?

It's a rhetorical question. That means you can answer it now in your mind or you can walk with me through this chapter as I make my case for the first option.

Once you're all set up in your leadership position and you've assembled your team, there's a couple of questions you need to answer.

WHAT DO WE NEED TO DO?

HOW ARE WE GOING TO DO IT?

Let's tackle the first question, *WHAT DO WE NEED TO DO?* This is a question about vision. Leadership is necessary when a group of people attempt to move together in a certain direction. The same direction. It may be coordinating an event, a cause, or a bunch of projects. It might be winning an award or competition.

The thing is, you need to know what it is this group needs to do to make that happen. Finding clarity around a certain direction can come in the form of goals, or objectives, or milestones. Basically, you need to be able to identify how to get from *here* to *there*.

Here is where you're currently at in the present moment.
There is where you want to be.

In order to move from *here* to *there*, you and your team have some work to do. Changes need to happen. Your hope and dream is to accomplish each task in a way that brings you closer to the different reality you have identified as *there*.

STAYING *HERE* DOESN'T REQUIRE LEADERSHIP. If a group of people want things to remain the same, accept the status quo, and do what they've always done they don't need much guidance.

GETTING TO *THERE* TAKES MOVEMENT. It takes action. And it needs leadership to always point toward *there* so everyone knows where they're going and do their best to go *there* together.

The second question is a strategic question, *HOW ARE WE GOING TO DO IT?* Once you identify the what, you need to consider the how. You have to figure out how you're going to lead your team.

You must decide what type of leader you are going to be as you move your team from *here* to *there*. There are probably as many unique leadership styles as there are leaders. But for the sake of this chapter, I am going to give you three of the more prominent choices.

You can be the type of leader who:

DEMANDS

MANIPULATES

SERVES

I know you're a clever reader and have already guessed which style I will advocate for (you did see the chapter title, didn't you?). But let's go ahead and take a look at the first two.

Leadership is often seen as a position of power (whether actual or perceived). You've probably seen or worked for people who have been placed in a leadership role and immediately assume this means they can tell people what to do. They makes demands based on the authority of the position they hold. They demand obedience. They demand work be done. They use their authority like a club. People submit because they have to.

Do you enjoy following leaders like that? Do you respect leaders like that?

My friend Ed Robinson says, "the only real use of power is to give it away." **Making demands based on the authority of one's position is one of the lowest forms of leadership.** It might accomplish what you are hoping for in the moment, but it will slowly dissolve the fabric of a team.

Sometimes people abuse the power of leadership through manipulation. Manipulative leaders often use guilt or shame to coerce people into action. They hold rewards or punishments over people's heads in order to get what they want. They play on the emotions and character of others, leaving people feeling used and abused.

The demanding or manipulative leader can have the same vision of what *there* looks like. But they slowly lose influence over the group because of the way they lead. People begin to feel mistreated. They go about getting to *there* in a completely different way than the third type of leader. This is the leader who serves.

A leader may need to be demanding in a time of crisis. There may be a moment when a leader needs to coerce someone to do the right thing. But it's the leader's overall style I'm addressing here. It's found in the one or two words those around you would use to describe your leadership (what would they say about you?).

WHEN YOU TRULY UNDERSTAND THAT LEADERSHIP IS NOT ABOUT YOU, YOUR BEST MOVE IS IN THE DIRECTION OF SERVING OTHERS. It is radically different than the demanding or manipulating leader.

Here are some of the characteristics I've identified in a leader who serves.

- A leader who serves puts the needs of the team members before his or her own.
- A leader who serves cares about people (not just what people can do).
- A leader who serves identifies what each person needs to do and helps him or her accomplish it.
- A leader who serves gives credit to the team instead of taking the credit for him or herself.

- A leader who serves offers encouragement and support to team members.
- A leader who serves is just as concerned with the journey toward the goal as he or she is with reaching the goal.
- A leader who serves wants his or her people to grow through the process of moving forward.
- A leader who serves will model serving in front of his or her team so that they might better learn to serve each other.
- A leader who serves sees serving as strength, not weakness.

Are you starting to see the paradox of leadership that's not about you? It flows out of a leader's motive.

The leaders who inspire aren't actually motivated to lead people; they are motivated to serve them.

It is a subtle twist of logic. People follow leaders because they know that the leader is looking out for them and their interests. By serving others, you will earn the loyalty and respect that leads to them serving you back.

✳ ✳ ✳
MEASURING PERCEPTIONS

One way to measure your effectiveness as a leader who serves is to get feedback from those around you. The following tool can be filled out by others to evaluate their own perceptions of your leadership.

You have my permission to make copies of this tool or to distribute it in some other manner. Hand it out to those whom you lead.

If you are leader who values excellence, than you won't fear evaluation.

Participants will rate you on a scale of 1 – 5, with 1=Strongly Disagree and 5=Strongly Agree.

. . . .

This person puts my best interests ahead of his/her own.

1   2   3   4   5

This person does everything he/she can to serve me.

1   2   3   4   5

This person sacrifices his/her own interests to meet my needs.

1   2   3   4   5

This person goes above and beyond the call of duty to meet my needs.

1   2   3   4   5

This person seems alert to what is happening.

1   2   3   4   5

This person is good at anticipating the consequences of decisions.

1   2   3   4   5

This person has great awareness of what is going on.

1   2   3   4   5

This person seems in touch with what's happening.

1   2   3   4   5

This person seems to know what is going to happen.

1   2   3   4   5

This person believes that the organization needs to play a moral role in society.

1   2   3   4   5

This person sees the organization for its potential to contribute to society.

1   2   3   4   5

This person encourages me toward a community spirit in the workplace.

1   2   3   4   5

This person is preparing the organization to make a positive difference in the future.

1   2   3   4   5

. . . .

Another way to use this tool is to fill it out for yourself and then compare it to the results you get from others. You can use your results as a way to engage others in conversation about their perceptions.

BUILDING COMMUNITY

If leadership is not about you, then who is it about?

IT'S ABOUT THEM. It's about the amazing group of people who have come together under a common purpose or cause. They want to accomplish something — something they can't accomplish by themselves.

In order to get from *here* to *there* it will require leadership. Your leadership.

You not only get to point them toward the goal, you get to guide them on the path that gets them *there*. **You get to create the kind of atmosphere, vibe, and culture that this group of people will exist in along the way.**

If you coach a basketball team, you know that practice is an important part of the journey toward a championship. If you are the president of a club, you know that your weekly meetings are an important part of the journey toward successful events.

If you oversee a group of people at work, you know that

anything you can do together outside of work will enhance the journey toward your success at work.

Lloyd Alexander said, "The journey is the treasure." Somewhere between *here* and *there*, those you lead can become something more than a group of individuals trying to accomplish a goal. They can become something better together than they could ever be alone.

They can become a community.

WEARING THE SAME T-SHIRT DOESN'T MAKE A GROUP OF PEOPLE A TEAM. Building community doesn't happen just by being in the same room together. It takes an intentional effort on the part of everyone. As the leader, you create space and opportunity for community to happen.

I can tell if a group is moving toward community by the way they set up the chairs. Some groups set the chairs up in rows. Rows create audiences. Some groups set the chairs up in circles. Circles create community.

There's a deep need in all of us. It is more powerful than the need to achieve. It's the need to belong.

You can't force community. You can't make people like each other. You can't demand that everyone trust the person sitting next to them. There is no quick formula to achieve community.

But there are certain elements that will encourage community to take place. There is a way to tap into the need to belong that we each possess.

1. TIME

Community takes time. It doesn't happen in a moment, but occurs with the accumulation of moments. This is why you need to find space and time for the group to focus on the people they work with apart from the work itself.

How are you creating space in the schedule for your group to build relationships?

2. VISION

Community grows as people work toward a common purpose or goal. A team is not just "a group of people."

A team is a group of people who own the same dream for a better future.

They are all headed in the same direction. People are more apt to work together if they know that those around them have committed themselves to the same effort.

What are you doing to communicate the vision with clarity on a regular basis?

3. SACRIFICE

The willingness of individuals to sacrifice their own time, resources, and energy for the good of others builds community. **Selfishness is one of the greatest barriers to growing community.** Apathy is a close second.

SACRIFICE IS CONTAGIOUS. When one person gives something up for the good of another, it inspires the same in others.

How can you acknowledge and celebrate the sacrifices group members make for each other?

4. INTERDEPENDENCE

The sense of community builds as people find themselves interdependent on others in the group. Interdependence is defined as *a mutually supportive relationship*.

It is greater than mere dependence and develops through a maturing trust in one another and a willingness to risk vulnerability. People open up to one another, becoming more authentic and transparent with the others in the group.

Interdependence creates a strong connection and commitment amongst group members. They accept and embrace one another. **They find ways to celebrate their individuality while transcending their differences.** This is what carries them through the difficult times.

Are you working toward something so challenging that it requires group members to be interdependent on each other in order to achieve it?

5. CONFLICT

If you are a leader who wants to create community with those around you, you won't shy away from conflict. You will work through it because you know it is a necessary building block of community. The strongest communities walk through conflict together.

> Conflict is necessary to move beyond superficiality.

Community is formed and strengthened as a group of people learn to disagree and debate gracefully. In the midst of problems and differences, they seek resolution by listening to each other and respecting one another. Conflict tests a group's ability to commit to struggle together rather than against one another.

How will you guide the group through conflict and disagreements?

WHEN A LEADER TRULY UNDERSTANDS THE POWER OF COMMUNITY, THE IDEA OF "LEADER" BECOMES LESS ABOUT A CERTAIN PERSON OR POSITION AND MORE ABOUT THE SPIRIT OF THE GROUP. Everyone takes responsibility and commits to lead through their unique contribution and giftedness.

Leadership becomes something that is embraced by each member of the community at different levels and at different times. It's the power of the community that has the greatest influence on the decisions that need to be made and the course of action necessary to move forward.

ME OR WE

There is a difference between the leader who is all about ME and the leader who is all about WE. I created two lists of words to describe those differences. Which words best describe your style of leadership?

ME	**WE**
Selfish	Selfless
Control	Collaborate
Alone	Together
Yours	Ours
Fearing	Trusting
Protect	Provide
Egotistical	Empathetic
Versus You	Values You
Exclusive	Shared
Take Credit	Give Credit
Finite	Infinite

Leadership starts with you, but it's not about you. It's about us (or rather, it's about WE). Instead of focusing on *WHAT CAN YOU DO FOR ME?* the focus shifts toward *WHAT CAN I DO FOR YOU?*

DELEGATION

You can't do everything by yourself and call yourself a leader.

If you do everything by yourself, you are not a leader — you are a worker.

One of the best ways to determine if you're more of a worker or a leader is to look at where you focus your time and attention. **The worker primarily focuses on tasks, the leader primarily focuses on people.**

I'm not saying a worker is bad and a leader is good. Both are necessary. Both are important. In fact, you might be a great worker. But that's not what you were elected or selected to be. You were given an opportunity because those around you needed a leader.

So how do you focus primarily on people? It means you look for ways to get others involved. You create space and you create opportunity. You don't try and do it all (the tasks) by yourself. You look for people who can jump in and help.

YOU START TO FUNCTION LIKE A LEADER WHEN YOU GIVE PART OF THE WORK AWAY. You let go of some of the tasks and empower others to complete them. You allow others to share in the responsibility of the work that needs to get done.

If you're behaving like a worker, it's time to change your perspective. You need to begin to see your role as a leader. This means you need to delegate. And delegation can be a tricky issue for any leader.

The word, "delegation" is derived from Latin and means *to send from*. Think about it; you are taking the time to send the work "from" you "to" someone else. Delegation is defined as giving others the authority to act on your behalf, accompanied with the initial responsibility and accountability for results. It's a process where you give someone else an opportunity to take on a task or project. The thing that makes delegation unique is that it is an opportunity that is offered, never demanded.

Great delegation lies somewhere between trying to hold on to every detail, unable to give anything away, versus being completely absent and lazy, avoiding any sense of responsibility for the work of others. In that wonderful "in-between" place lies the chance to offer others expanded responsibilities…with a safety net. You are involved in the process. Handled effectively, delegation allows others to grow in their experience and not live in fear of failure.

If you're in a leadership role, you can delegate as much or as little of your work as you please. The thing about delegation is you still retain the ultimate responsibility for the completion of the work.

Delegation simply allows you to pass the authority on as necessary to complete a task or project, but the obligation to see it completed still rests on your shoulders.

A lot of leaders (who are actually workers) will shy away from delegation because they're afraid someone will say no. This fear is one of the reasons we think it's easier to do it all by ourselves.

Another reason we might not delegate certain tasks is because we don't want to give up control. Or maybe it's because we can't figure out who to ask.

Simply put, workers will *do* where leaders will *delegate*.

I've compiled some delegation wisdom you can apply to your leadership. Improving your delegation skills will improve your effectiveness as a leader. Use this list to develop your own philosophy and process for delegating work to others.

1. Look at delegation as an opportunity for growth. Others grow through the process. Your leadership grows as you focus more on people than tasks.

2. Delegation provides you with more time to work on projects that only you, as the leader, should be working on.

3. Delegation is more meaningful when others see the benefit of completing a task.

4. When you describe the outcome you are hoping for, you allow people to use their creativity more than if you provided a step-by-step guide to completion.

5. Clarify any limits a person may have with completing a task or project. Let them know the extent of the authority you're giving them.

6. Delegated tasks done with excellence turn into greater opportunities for involvement, promotion, and recognition in the future.

7. DELEGATION EXERCISE: Make a list of all of the activities you do on a regular or routine basis. Which ones can someone else do?

8. Challenge others to reach their potential when delegating. Encourage them to stretch their capabilities. Expect them to succeed, and you will be pleasantly surprised more frequently than not.

9. Teach those you delegate to be problem-solvers and not problem-reporters. If someone reports a problem, expect them to come with two or three solutions to consider as well.

10. Smaller tasks should be given to someone to prove he or she is capable. Larger tasks or complete projects should be given to someone who has proven he or she is responsible.

11. Talk about what an outcome of excellence looks like at the beginning. Don't surprise people with evaluation they weren't planning for. Clearly define objectives and

outcomes in measurable terms. Expectations must be lined out at the beginning.

12. You can delegate a task to someone and he or she can say "no."

13. Delegate the parts of your position that you are weak in to others who have strengths in that area.

14. Delegation has a dark side. It might take longer. You might actually have done it better. But leadership doesn't take back a delegated item for that reason. Part of your leadership responsibility is helping others learn to do it better.

15. Don't surprise people by checking in randomly. Let them know up front how often you plan on asking for updates and keep communication lines open.

16. Delegation strengthens your leadership. It shows you are doing your job by getting others involved and getting results with and through others.

17. When you delegate, there is always the risk that someone will make a mistake. But people often learn the

most from the mistakes they make. Leaders aren't as upset by mistakes as much as repeated mistakes. Since we all make mistakes, help people to learn and grow from them.

18. Delegation happens most effectively when you match the requirements of the assignment with talents of the person.

19. People have greater buy-in and invest more effort when they feel the freedom to use their own creative ideas and energy to accomplish a delegated task than if a supervisor tells them how to do it.

20. DELEGATION EXERCISE: Who are three people you could ask to assist you with a project you're working on?

21. Effective delegation requires mutual trust. You trust the capabilities of others. They trust that they are doing something meaningful and significant.

22. Follow up. Follow up. Follow up. Don't hand off the project or task and then ask about it the day before it's due.

23. Set expectations, responsibility, outcomes, resources,

and accountability in place. Try not to step in when someone faces a problem. Allow others to learn from their experience. You will be tempted to step in too soon.

24. Asking for help doesn't mean you're helpless. It gives someone else the chance to be helpful.

25. DELEGATION EXERCISE: Here are some great questions to ask at your first follow-up meeting:

Is there anything I can do for you?

Are there any questions you have?

Are there any tools you need?

Does everything about this make sense?

26. What else would you add to this list?

_____

THE "T" IN TEAM STANDS FOR TRUST

I walked into the room full of newly elected student leaders. You could feel the excitement. You could sense that each one of them was motivated to do his or her very best. They all wore the same t-shirt. They were all on the same team. The only question that remained between their success or failure as a group was a simple one...

Would they learn to trust each other?

Every new year is full of excitement and anticipation. But the one big difference between the teams that overcome the obstacles and the ones who get blown apart by the barriers is found in one basic characteristic — trust.

Trust is the foundation of effective teams.

Patrick Lencioni, in one of the best leadership books for teams, *The Five Dysfunctions Of A Team*, states the following: "Remember teamwork begins by building trust. And the only way to do that is to overcome our need for invulnerability."

You may have charisma, outstanding talents, the ability to communicate well, and the most capable team on the planet. **But if the people on your team don't trust you or trust each other, you'll never achieve the things you set out to accomplish.**

INSPIRE TRUST AND YOU'LL INCREASE MORALE. Trust reduces frustration and skepticism. Where there is trust, teams tend to stay together. When there is no trust, teams tend to fracture. Trust will raise the level of your team's effectiveness.

Wearing the same jersey or uniform doesn't guarantee trust. Trust is not automatic. It doesn't come with the title you were elected or selected to bear. You must earn trust — from day one — and every day after that.

Here are six ways I believe you can earn and build trust with others. They are not quick fix remedies. It's not about doing it once. These are lifestyle behaviors that will earn the trust of teammates. Each one is a pathway to greater trust when used properly.

1. BE VULNERABLE.

I'm always amazed at the response I get when I share my biggest mistakes with other people. I don't do it for pity. I do it because I want people to know who I am and who I am becoming as a result of the mistakes I've made.

Patrick Lencioni talks about the value of vulnerability later in his book, "Great teams do not hold back with one another. They are unafraid to air their dirty laundry. They admit their mistakes, their weaknesses, and their concerns without fear of reprisal."

When I am real and authentic with people, they are more willing to be open and honest with me about where they are at in life.

> People aren't looking for a leader who is perfect, they're looking for one who is honest.

2. TAKE RESPONSIBILITY FOR THE CONSEQUENCES OF TEAM DECISIONS.

Responsibility is the greatest requirement of leadership. When a decision goes right, the leader should be quick to praise the people around him or her who helped make it happen. When a decision goes wrong, the first person to take responsibility should be the leader. Point the finger at yourself at the point of failure and you will earn the respect of those around you.

So many people want to place blame on anyone and anything other than themselves. A leader who takes responsibility for both decision and consequence is rare.

3. COACH PEOPLE UP...NOT DOWN.

When you witness someone making a mistake or moving in a wrong direction you have a choice in how you'll respond. You can berate or belittle this person or you can inspire and motivate this person to do better.

We have all been under the guidance of someone who pushed us to do our best without making us feel inferior. Every time you correct someone you have the opportunity to increase their belief in themselves as well as improve their behavior.

4. RESPOND WELL TO FAILURE.

Whether you like it or not, you are an example to others. You get to choose each day what type of example you will be. Your example shines through in both success and failure. Everyone will experience failure. That includes you. Once you admit that, it's only a matter of deciding how you will respond to your failures.

A healthy response involves acknowledging the failure and learning from what went wrong.

When you constantly repeat the same failure over and over, it only tells us that you're not paying attention.

When you respond appropriately to your failure, you give those around you permission to learn from their failure. If you try to hide your failure, you only frustrate those around you who are well aware and wish you'd been more honest with them and with yourself.

5. MAKE ROOM FOR DISCUSSION, NOT DIVISION.

I hope you haven't created a team of people who agree on everything and see life from the same perspective as you. If that's the case, you've put together a very boring and myopic team.

When you gather people of diverse viewpoints and ideas, you create opportunities for innovation and immense creativity.

Different perspectives can be a great asset if you don't allow them to divide your team.

This is why it's important to create space for discussion. You want to allow people to be heard and appreciated. If your first response is to judge others because their view is different than your own, you will limit the potential of your team.

You will know that you have begun to build trust on your team when you move beyond *acknowledging* the differences between each member and begin *appreciating* those differences and what they contribute to the team.

6. FIND THE GOLD.

Having lived in Northern California for a period of my life, I know a little bit about mining for gold. It is a tedious process. As in most mining efforts, you have to move a lot of dirt. Nobody is looking for or celebrating the dirt because there is so much of it. The goal is to find the gold.

EFFECTIVE LEADERS RECOGNIZE THE SPECIAL AND UNIQUE GIFTEDNESS IN EACH PERSON. Every person can make a contribution. Your job is to find ways to incorporate these gifts for the betterment of the team and the accomplishment of your goals.

People can grow frustrated by a lack of progress or

improvement. But you are on the lookout for those glimpses of greatness and potential in others. Sometimes those on your team can't see past all of the dirt in their lives. The dirt is the mundane, ordinary, average, and day-to-day stuff that keeps us from reaching our true potential. You will earn their trust when they see you are dedicated to pointing out the potential that lies hidden within them.

THE "T" IN TEAM STANDS FOR TRUST (PART 2)

Maybe you've heard this one.

Question: Why should you never trust the world's fastest animal?

Answer: Because he's a cheetah.

I know it's a corny joke. But it helps me make my point (which justifies putting that joke in the book). There are behaviors that build trust and there are behaviors that kill trust. Cheating is a trust killer.

If you get caught cheating, lying, stealing, deceiving, or doing something similar to these, trust is broken. It can happen in a moment.

BUT THERE ARE BEHAVIORS THAT BUILD TRUST. These take time. They are daily investments in the "trust bank." The key is consistency.

1. GO FIRST.
Going first is often seen as a leadership trait. You go first

to set an example. You gain influence as you provide an example worth following. You model what trust looks like when you step into the circle of trust before anyone else.

You set the example for others by being the first to extend trust. It takes courage and vulnerability to trust someone else. That's what makes it so powerful when it happens. Trust helps a team accomplish so much more than they could without it. But it's fragile. It's not based on certainty. Much like faith, trust is a risk. Your example demonstrates that trusting each other is worth the risk.

YOUR EXAMPLE SETS THE TONE AND BEGINS TO MODEL A CULTURE THAT VALUES TRUSTING ONE ANOTHER. It can be as simple as looking across the table at the members of your team and telling them, "I trust you."

It's in our nature to respond positively to positive input (google "mirror neurons"). So if someone tells you, *I trust you*, there's something that clicks inside of us making us more likely to trust that person. Think of it as inner reciprocation. Of course, it works the opposite way as well. Tell someone, *I don't trust you*, and I'm pretty sure that person will lean toward not trusting you either.

This same phenomenon occurs when you tell someone you believe in them or you depend on them or you need them.

PEOPLE MAY NOT KNOW WHAT TRUST LOOKS AND FEELS LIKE UNTIL YOU MODEL IT FOR THEM. When you go first, you put a picture in people's mind of a trusting person. You set the example for them to follow.

2. BE WORTH TRUSTING.

If the people on your team are going to go out on a limb for you, they have to decide if it's worth the risk. Every word, action, and behavior you demonstrate (especially in times of difficulty) will help or hinder another person's decision about whether or not to trust you.

If you and I want to be trusted, we must honestly look at ourselves and ask: Am I worth trusting?

Think of it this way, if I asked the people on your team who the most trusting person is on the team, would your name be mentioned? If not, why not?

TRUST TAKES TIME TO BUILD. It's earned in the same way one earns respect. People know where you stand. They recognize a consistent pattern to your life. In each and every interaction, the scales are slowly tipped in favor of trust. People see you as a reliable person and not a risky relationship.

Trust is worth something. It's valuable. It takes an investment on both sides of the relationship. You choose to live in a "trustworthy" manner because you don't want to lose the trust others place in you as the leader. Once trust is lost, it's difficult to earn it back.

3. TAKE RESPONSIBILITY FOR THE CONSEQUENCES OF YOUR CHOICES.

If I could define leadership in one word (besides the word leadership) it would be responsibility. The reason I choose that word is because I believe that's where leadership starts and ends.

A person doesn't start off deciding to be a leader, a person begins by deciding to be responsible.

Responsibility is also one of the most practical ways for you and I to build trust with those around us. Leaders take responsibility. They take responsibility for themselves and they take responsibility for the good of others.

I'll refer to Lencioni's words once more concerning trust and responsibility: "What exactly does vulnerability-based trust look like in practice? It is evident among team members who say things to one another like 'I screwed up,' 'I was wrong,' 'I need help,' 'I'm sorry,' and 'You're better than I am at this.' Most important, they only make one of these statements when they mean it, and especially when they really don't want to."

I've seen it time and again, a leader takes responsibility at the front end of a project or cause. But when something goes wrong, he or she won't take responsibility for the consequences. Every choice has a consequence. We show we are worth trusting when we take responsibility for both the choice and the consequence of that choice.

TAKE RESPONSIBILITY FOR THE GOOD OF OTHERS

Leadership starts with taking responsibility. In the last chapter I said, *Leaders take responsibility for themselves and they take responsibility for the good of others.* In other words, leadership starts with you but it's not about you. It's about working for the good of others.

Imagine the following scenario: You walk into your house and your mom or dad is standing over a broken lamp on the floor. They look at the lamp and then they look at you. Their eyes dart back and forth between the lamp and you. Their gaze is somewhat accusing. Their look is asking the unspoken question.

But you've been gone all day. You don't know anything about the details of the broken lamp. So you speak up in the awkward silence with the response that every child has spoken since the dawn of time.

I didn't do it.

You don't want to be blamed for something you didn't do.

You don't want to get involved in a mess that's not your fault. You shy away from anything that will put you in the middle of the situation.

But that's not what leaders do. In fact, they do the opposite. They take responsibility.

When you choose to be a leader, you forfeit your right to forfeit responsibility.

You put your rights on hold and take responsibility.

- You willingly step into situations that need fixing even though you did nothing to break them.
- You willingly move into matters that require the assistance of someone else.
- You willingly probe into problems that others are unwilling or unable to solve.

Let's go back to the broken lamp. The initial response for most people focuses on themselves: "I didn't do it." The leadership response is one of responsibility for the good of others. It says, "How can I help you clean that up?"

Taking responsibility for the good of others is a willingness to be a part of the solution in the lives of others rather than the problem.

When you begin to look at each situation through the lens of responsibility, you'll see opportunities to make a difference. You can impact any situation when you approach it with the mindset that you will:

ADD VALUE

PUT THE NEEDS OF OTHERS BEFORE YOUR OWN.

When you do both of those things, you grow your influence with others.

It's when we take responsibility for the good of others that we truly earn the right to be called a leader.

Not because we take that title for ourselves, but because others recognize it in us and choose to follow.

H.E.R.O. OR H.E.R.M.?

I love a good superhero movie.

I am especially intrigued by the stories that show how an ordinary person becomes a superhero. Most superheroes are born out of necessity. There is a crisis that occurs that is too big for "ordinary" people to handle. It's a super problem that requires a superhero.

When I'm training a group of students, I will often ask them a simple question:

If you could have any superhero power you imagine, what would it be?

The answers are typical: the ability to fly, to be invisible, super-strength, super speed, and my favorite — the ability to pick a perfect melon in the produce section of the grocery store.

I love asking this question because it gets everyone talking. Everyone can imagine what it would be like to have some type of superpower. Maybe that's why we love superhero movies so much. We all wonder what it would be like to do something extra-ordinary.

As we share our answers to the question, I follow up by asking what people would do with their superpowers. Everyone begins to visualize how much easier their life would be if they had this special gift. They imagine how fun it would be to use their power for themselves. They think about how much attention they would get.

This makes them all villains.

When I state that out loud, the room grows quiet. Nobody wants to be the villain. But it's true.

IN EVERY SUPERHERO MOVIE, THERE IS OFTEN A FINE LINE BETWEEN THE HERO AND THE VILLAIN. But you can figure it out pretty quickly which side of the line a person with superpowers stands on.

The hero will always be the person who puts the needs of others before his or her own.

The superhero uses his or her abilities for the good of others.

The villains use their powers for the good of themselves.

The words "hero" and "leader" have something in common. They are both titles given to someone by others. Real heroes, just like real leaders, don't start off trying to be those things. They simply took responsibility for needs other than their own. They made a sacrifice that turned ordinary into extra-ordinary.

In the real world, none of us have much in the way of superpowers. We can't fly, we can't be invisible, and we can't see through walls. But that doesn't mean we're powerless.

We are surrounded by need. There are problems that need solving. Where are our heroes?

Perhaps this can be a phone booth moment for you. You just might be the person we need. You have been given abilities, resources, and perspectives you can use "for the good of others." When you truly see that it's not about you, you are more ready to become the H.E.R.O. those around you have been looking for.

I created an acrostic to demonstrate the potential each

of us has to be a H.E.R.O. to the people and situations we encounter.

Help

You can make an immediate impact in any situation. Don't believe me? See what happens when you let these four words be the first thing out of your mouth: How can I help?

Problems and difficulties tend to isolate us. People around you need to know they're not alone. Be helpful and you'll break down barriers and build relationships.

Encourage

To encourage someone is to actually give them courage. You share your courage because people have lost theirs and can't see past their problems.

Despair and discouragement can blind those around you from knowing what they're capable of. They have the ability but they lack the courage. Encouragement heals a faulty perspective.

Rescue

We will always need heroes because there will always be people who need saving. Your leadership position is a platform. You can use the tools, resources, and influence at your disposal to make someone else's life better.

HEROES DON'T TYPICALLY RUN AROUND LOOKING FOR EXTRA-ORDINARY MOMENTS TO BE HEROIC. They simply prepare themselves in the ordinary, day-to-day moments. When a need presents itself, they're ready to step in.

We often hear someone who has been labeled a hero respond by saying, *I was just doing my job*.

OTHERS

This is what ties the whole thing together. It is using your ability to help, encourage, and rescue for the good of others. That's what it means to be heroic.

Don't believe me?

When a person only helps himself, we call him *selfish*.

When a person only encourages himself,
we call him a *bragger* or *proud*.

When a person only rescues himself,
we call him a *coward*.

If you only look out for you, then you are a H.E.R.M. Someone who helps, encourages, and rescues ME.

H.E.R.M.S ARE THE VILLAINS IN ALL OF THE GOOD STORIES. They have what's necessary to save the world but only want to save themselves. They have all the qualities of a hero but they choose selfish over selfless.

Focusing on ME doesn't make one a good hero. It definitely doesn't make for a good leader.

SOLVE PROBLEMS

Everyone has problems.

If you ever wonder why you have problems, do the following: check to see if you're breathing. If you are breathing, then you'll have problems. That's the only requirement. People who aren't breathing don't have problems.

Problems are the normal part of life. To live a life that is free from problems is not normal.

Problems occur for a lot of different reasons. They typically fall into one of three categories:

    a. You cause them.

    b. Someone else causes them.

    c. They cause themselves.

LEADERS AREN'T AFRAID OF PROBLEMS. They may not like them, but they don't fear them. **Problems are a leader's job security.** If there weren't any problems, we wouldn't need you to be a leader.

Leadership starts with you when you do the hard work necessary to solve your own problems. But when you take the next step, when you realize that leadership is not about you, you actually start looking for ways to assist others in solving problems as well.

A LEADER'S PERSPECTIVE TOWARD PROBLEMS IS THE FIRST STEP TOWARD ACTUALLY SOLVING A PROBLEM. **Right perspective gives you a better chance at right solutions.** Without the right perspective the progress of your team can be halted and conflict can easily escalate. Noted psychiatrist and author, Theodore Rubin said, "The problem is not that there are problems. The problem is expecting otherwise and thinking that having problems is a problem."

One of the ways to figure out your perspective is to ask yourself: *How do I feel about problems?*

How you feel about problems impacts how you face problems.

Before you start to solve a problem, you need to understand your perspective of the problem. Your perspective basically boils down to two choices: **You can see problems as obstacles to be avoided or opportunities to be embraced.**

YOUR PERSPECTIVE IS YOUR SECRET WEAPON. It's also the number one determining factor toward your ability to solve problems. The words, "I can't" are typically a self-fulfilling prophecy.

If you view problems as walls too big to climb, they probably will be. But if you see problems as opportunities to grow, change, think, flex, and work together — you have conquered the most difficult part of the problem solving process.

If you don't see problems as opportunities, you'll see them as obstacles and will be tempted to implement one or all of the following flawed strategies:

RUN FROM THE PROBLEM.

IGNORE THE PROBLEM.

COMPLAIN ABOUT THE PROBLEM.

None of those strategies will help you accomplish the very thing we need you to help us do as the leader — SOLVE THE PROBLEM.

All of the greatest inventions in our world came about as the result of trying to solve a problem. Advances in science, cures for disease, technological breakthroughs, and the birth of nations were the result of problem solving. The problems were the doorway to opportunity.

Take a minute and look at the following chart. A wrong perspective will choke you while a right perspective will challenge you. Which perspective do you have?

<u>**A Right Perspective**</u>	<u>**A Wrong Perspective**</u>
Problems are solvable	Problems are unsolvable
Problems are temporary	Problems are permanent
Problems are a part of life	Problems not a part of life
Problems make us better	Problems make us bitter
Problems challenge us	Problems control us
Problems stretch us	Problems stop us

As the leader, you set the tone for the way your team will approach each problem.

> The way you describe and talk about problems demonstrates the perspective you want each member of your team to possess.

Leaders aren't surprised by problems because a leader is prepared for them. Part of your preparation for problem-solving will be developing the right perspective right now. Leaders develop the right perspective before problems occur.

Here are five questions that can aid you in your preparation. They won't necessarily solve your problem. But they will shape your perspective about the problem. They will get you thinking about the way you handle problems, as well as your approach toward solving them.

1. WHAT DO I NEED TO DO DIFFERENTLY TO SOLVE THIS PROBLEM?

If anyone knew something about problems, it was Albert Einstein. He said, "We can't solve problems by using the same kind of thinking we used when we created them." Einstein knew that something needed to change if the problem was going to be solved.

For Einstein, it meant changing his thinking (perspective). If there is a problem, something needs to change. Start with yourself.

2. WHAT DO I NEED TO DO TO BE THE RIGHT KIND OF PERSON IN THE MIDST OF THIS PROBLEM?

This is a character issue. You may not find an immediate

solution to your problem. You may not have control or influence on what's causing the problem. You may not like what the problem is causing.

Whatever the situation, the one thing you do have control over is yourself. **In most cases, problems and crisis have a way of exposing who we really are.** But they also provide an opportunity to deepen and strengthen our character if we are focused on it. Allow the process of working through a problem to be an opportunity to truly see "what you're made of."

3. WHAT IS KEEPING ME FROM SOLVING THIS PROBLEM?

If you ask this question, you might quickly discover that it's your perspective of the problem that is in your way. Or maybe it's the way you've identified the problem. The point of this question is to identify the obstacles that keep you from being a problem-solver.

4. WHAT WILL SOLVING THIS PROBLEM MAKE POSSIBLE?

This is a vision question.

Sometimes people won't solve a problem because they have grown comfortable living with the problem.

This question gets you thinking about the opportunities that are out there if you didn't have this problem standing in your way. This is a great question to ask those around you who are hesitant to change. It can encourage people to tackle a problem for the purpose of a better and brighter future.

5. WHAT KIND OF STORY DO I WANT TO TELL A YEAR FROM NOW ABOUT THIS PROBLEM?

History is full of case studies on the different ways people handled their problems. This question encourages you to work through your problem in a way that can teach and train others who may face similar difficulties.

One of the saddest stories you can tell is a tale filled with regret. How would you feel if a year from now you're facing the same problem because you failed to do something about it right now? That's a depressing story.

LEARN TO FACE YOUR PROBLEMS WITH AN EYE TOWARD OPPORTUNITY. Set an example for those around you by modeling the right perspective towards problems. Those problems are the very reason why your leadership is necessary.

THE HANDWRITTEN
THANK YOU NOTE

I am on a crusade to revive the handwritten thank you note.

In a world of texting, email, twitter, and facebook status updates, the handwritten thank you note has become somewhat of a relic.

But this old-fashioned symbol of gratitude will make a profound difference in the lives of those around you.

When someone receives a handwritten note from you, they immediately know you took the time to write specifically to them. It's easy to copy and paste emails or text. But when you pen a handwritten thank you note, it contains your personal gratitude DNA.

Handwritten is original every time. Your penmanship (as sloppy as it is) is unique. Your writing is your own. When you send a handwritten thank you note, you offer a word of encouragement in a way that no one else can. They are remarkably personal.

A little more time and energy makes a huge impact. Handwritten is more meaningful than typed-out because it's rare.

People hold on to them. I've seen handwritten thank you notes I've written show up on people's bulletin boards. I have a file folder that I keep of encouraging notes that have meant the world to me. These things have a long and strong shelf life.

They convey a sense of relationship, as well as gratitude.

A handwritten thank you note tells someone else that he or she is worth the extra time.

It conveys a higher level of sincerity and significance. Will you join me in my crusade?

It's easy. Buy a bunch of blank index cards and jot an encouraging note to one person each day this week. You can easily knock this out in 5-10 minutes each day. You can hand it to them, but it's even better if you mail it. Receiving a handwritten thank you note in the mail is the stuff of legends!

GO THE "EXTRA" MILE

THE ABILITY TO TRULY SERVE ANOTHER PERSON IS MORE POWERFUL WHEN IT OCCURS FREELY AND NOT OUT OF OBLIGATION.

It happens when service flows out of a true desire to serve another person. It is when a person serves, not because he or she has to or needs to, but because that person wants to.

This type of service expects nothing in return. The act of service becomes a gift this person is giving to another.

I believe this is exactly what the principle of "going the extra mile" is all about. The phrase *going the extra mile* (or the second mile) originated from the Bible (in the first book of the New Testament).

The specific passage is the words of Jesus, instructing a group of people gathered on a hillside to do the following: "If anyone forces you to go one mile, go with them two miles." (Matthew 5:41, NIV)

This is not simply a challenge to get more exercise. It's a subversive command to help a powerless people see they have all the resources they need to make a difference in the world.

In the days when this passage was written, Roman law dictated that a person was required to carry the pack of a Roman Centurion for one mile. Most of the time, those required to carry the pack were from the parts of society that were continually oppressed and disenfranchised under the Roman rule of law. They were forced to carry the Centurion's pack for a mile (because it was the law) and they knew they had to do it (or risk death in their disobedience).

The law was strict. When a person came to the end of one mile, he or she was under no further obligation. At this point, the Roman Centurion would release the person from having to carry the pack (because he or she had fulfilled what the law required).

It is at this precise moment where the idea of true service became more powerful than the law.

If a person chose to carry the pack of the Centurion for an

extra mile, this person did so out of freedom, not obligation or coercion.

It was unexpected. It was counter-cultural. It changed the entire dynamic of the situation. Suddenly, the person who *chose* to carry the pack went from inferior to influential. **It was his or her willingness to serve beyond the obligation of the law that proved more powerful than power itself.**

While the current culture of our day looks a lot different than it did in first century Rome, we have an opportunity to be the kind of leader who is willing to *go the extra mile* for those around us.

The challenge is for us to figure out how to engage in those opportunities where we can serve others because we choose to believe that's the best way to lead and live with each other in this world.

If you're a leader and you want to be a good one, your job is to help those around you be good at their job.

This doesn't mean doing their work for them; it means helping them get the resources and the information they need for them to perform their own jobs as well as they can. It also means watching their back and helping them fix mistakes when they make them. The more you do that, the more you offer your help because you want to, the more you will earn their trust so when you need them to go the extra mile for you, they will — gladly. Not because you're their boss, but because they respect and trust you.

How can you serve those around you in a way that demonstrates you *want to*, rather than serving because you *have to* or *need to*?

HOW'S YOUR SERVE?

Most people who serve in a leadership position got there through an election or selection process. But that process isn't enough to make someone a leader. A person must also go through a reflection process.

In order to do what a leader does you must learn to think like a leader thinks.

Learning to think like a leader is similar to the work a detective does at a crime scene. Always looking for clues and aware of the little things that can make a huge difference in how things turn out.

SADLY, THERE ARE MORE LEADERS WHO WANT TO LEAD BECAUSE OF WHAT THEY GET RATHER THAN WHAT THEY GET TO DO. Leadership is not just about leading, it's about serving. True leaders show up to give — and when circumstances require them to give more than they ever thought they would have to, they do so willingly.

As we're getting near the end of this book, I'd like you to invest in some reflection time. Leaders who serve because they want to have prepared their hearts and minds to respond in this way.

We can all benefit from an honest assessment of our attitudes and our actions in relation to serving those around us. If we only serve others when we feel like it, we let our fickle moods and attitudes dictate our ability to lead our people. If we only serve others when we stand to benefit, our people will see through our disingenuous actions and we'll damage any trust that we've built over time.

However, if we serve our team with the right attitude and with actions that are focused on "them," we'll earn our teammates' trust and loyalty, and we'll model the true meaning of servanthood.

It's time for the gut check. Take a look at each of the following statements. Rate each one on a scale of 1 - 10. 1 = I do this poorly, 10 = I do this extremely well.

YOUR ATTITUDE TOWARD SERVING:

You take action even when you don't "feel" like serving.
1   2   3   4   5   6   7   8   9   10

Your mood for the day doesn't effect your desire to serve others.

1   2   3   4   5   6   7   8   9   10

You believe all individual are deserving of your service.

1   2   3   4   5   6   7   8   9   10

You have the confidence to humble yourself and serve others.

1   2   3   4   5   6   7   8   9   10

You are you willing to serve even if no one will notice.

1   2   3   4   5   6   7   8   9   10

You plan to serve without the expectation of the favor being returned.

1   2   3   4   5   6   7   8   9   10

YOUR ACTIONS IN SERVING:

You are open to serving others even when it will inconvenience you.

1   2   3   4   5   6   7   8   9   10

You are willing to take risks that will benefit others but won't benefit you.

1   2   3   4   5   6   7   8   9   10

You first consider how your actions will impact your team before you consider the impact on you.

1   2   3   4   5   6   7   8   9   10

Leading your people comes before getting your work done.

1   2   3   4   5   6   7   8   9   10

You model servanthood in a way that encourages those around you to serve as well.

1   2   3   4   5   6   7   8   9   10

. . . .

Take a minute to reflect on your responses. What can you do to improve in one area today? What will it take to rate yourself one number higher?

GREATER THAN ONE

Every time I'm tempted to try and do my work all by myself, I'm reminded of this statement:

One is too small a number for greatness.

When you are all by yourself, the only person you can lead is yourself. I hope you will start there. I've seen too many people in leadership positions self-sabotage their efforts because they didn't do that part of leadership well. Leadership truly does start with you.

IF YOU WANT TO DO ANYTHING OF SIGNIFICANCE, IT WILL TAKE THE EFFORT OF MORE THAN ONE PERSON. It will take a team of people who are dedicated to heading in the same direction, striving to get from *here* to *there*.

That effort will also require leadership. And leadership isn't easy. You probably already know that.

In fact, since you've made it to the end of this book, here's what I think is true about you...

You already know it could get really difficult but you choose to put yourself out there anyway. You've got something inside of you that is stronger than any obstacle, opposition, or struggle.

You actually believe you can make a difference.

You want to lead because you can make things better. You love people and you love your organization. You have what it takes to do something meaningful and significant in the lives of others. You have an idea of a better future and you want to include as many people as you can in achieving it.

In every difficult situation, you are able to focus on what's most important. It's your dedication and drive and desire that motivates you through the obstacles and pushes you forward. If this was only something you did to build your resumé you'd be out the door at the first sign of trouble.

This isn't about awards or accolades or personal glory for you. It's not about being able to boss others around or get people to like you.

You want to lead because you want to give back and you

want to move forward.

LEADERSHIP ISN'T FOR EVERYONE. But it is for those who step into it for the right reasons. Those who do it for the good of others and the good of their organization will be much better equipped to weather the difficulties.

Those on your team and the people around you want you to lead well. They want to get from *here* to *there*. They also hope you'll be the type of leader who puts the needs of WE ahead of the needs of ME.

They want you to guide them by serving them. They are ready to give their energy to a leader who says, "Follow me, I'm right behind you all the way!"

Your team is watching how you live and lead through the paradox — leading yourself first but not making leadership about yourself. As you model this through your attitudes and actions, you'll earn their respect and admiration because you choose to lean into selflessness and not selfishness.

LEADERSHIP ISN'T ABOUT HAVING A TITLE NEAR THE TOP OF AN ORGANIZATIONAL CHART. It's not about holding a position of power over others. It's about setting the best example of what it takes to move a group of people from *here* to *there* by focusing mostly on others and only minimally on yourself.

DON'T CALL YOURSELF A LEADER. Work hard to ensure that everyone feels like they're working *with* you and not *for* you. When you consistently serve the needs of others with the right motives, then you'll be recognized as a leader.

"Leader" isn't a title you give yourself. It's an honor given to you by others.

✳ ✳ ✳
ACKNOWLEDGEMENTS

Every day I want to say *thank you* to someone. Today I'm especially grateful to those who have encouraged me in the process of writing this book.

I want to thank the student leaders who I work with each year. They inspire me with their energy and commitment to make things awesome for their peers.

I want to express my gratitude to the "upstairs" gang — Carey, Karen, Kenton, & Ronda — my friends and co-workers. We have partnered together in developing students for many years. Thank you for walking with me through the highs and lows.

I want to thank Kathy Burns and Sharon Stallings for their help with editing and clarity. Special thanks to Grant Miller for helping me with the study guide. And loving appreciation to Angie, who, when I count my blessings...I count you twice.

ABOUT THE AUTHOR

Tim Milburn currently serves as the Director of Campus Life at Northwest Nazarene University, located just outside of Boise, Idaho. He is the founder of Lifelong Leaders — an organization that inspires people to take responsibility, develop relationships, and achieve results.

Having worked with students for more than 25 years, Tim continually writes, speaks, and creates resources for student leaders and for those involved in the work of student leadership development.

When he's not developing lifelong leaders, Tim dabbles in graphic design, is a regular at Starbucks, and loves to tell a good story.

To continue the conversation...
   On the web: timmilburn.com
   On email: timothymilburn@gmail.com
   On twitter: @timage
   On facebook: facebook.com/timage

Made in the USA
Charleston, SC
20 May 2014